About the Book

From the first Jane Goodall was fascinated by animals. She brought home grubby worms and unfamiliar insects to ask her mother questions. Even as a small girl, she wrote down what she found out. She knew that when she grew up, she wanted to work with animals.

Jane was to have her dream when she went into the jungles of Tanzania in Africa to study chimpanzees in the wild. First she had to be accepted by them. Patiently she waited until the chimps got to know her. Affectionately, she gave them names—old Mr. McGregor with his balding head, raggedy-eared Flo, and fluffy-haired Olly, David Graybeard, big, strong Goliath, and lively baby Fifi.

Jane watched the chimps carefully and wrote down everything she saw. Some of her observations had never been known before, and her discoveries were recognized as important contributions by scientists around the world. She continues to study other animals and to share her findings with us.

Jane Goodall

by Eleanor Coerr
drawings by Kees de Kiefte

G.P. Putnam's Sons · New York

Library of Congress Cataloging in Publication Data
Coerr, Eleanor. JANE GOODALL.
(See and read biography)
SUMMARY: A biography of the woman whose childhood
love of wildlife led her into the African bush to study
chimpanzees and into later becoming a world-famous
ethologist.
1. Lawick-Goodall, Jane, Barones van—Juvenile
literature. [1. Lawick-Goodall, Jane, Barones van.
2. Naturalists. 3. Chimpanzees—Habits and behavior]
I. De Kiefte, Kees. II. Title.
QL31.L38C63 1975   591'.092'4 [B] [92]   75-32503
ISBN 0-399-20504-7   ISBN 0-399-60994-6 lib. bdg.

Jane Goodall

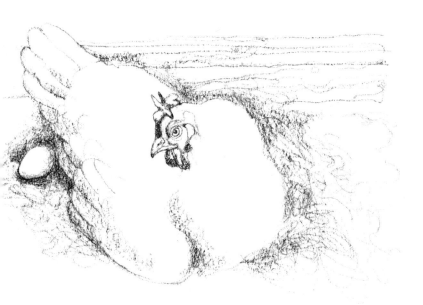

"Jane! Where are you?" Mrs. Goodall called to her daughter. "It's too late to play hide-and-seek." She had been calling Jane for a long time.

But four-year-old Jane was not playing a game. She was sitting very still in a neighbor's stuffy hen house hugging her toy chimpanzee, Jubilee. Earlier that day Jane had made up her mind to see how hens lay eggs. Hour after hour she waited. At last a hen laid an egg. Jane stared at its perfect, smooth shape. Then she rushed home to tell her mother about it.

Jane's life began on April 3, 1934. When she was three, a baby sister, Judy, was born. As soon as Jane could walk, she brought things into the house to show her mother. Sometimes it was a frog or bug. Other times it was a handful of grubby worms. Mrs. Goodall helped Jane learn about them all. She wanted her daughters to share her own love of nature.

By the time she was eight Jane knew much about the wildlife around her home in the seaside city of Bournemouth, England. In the daytime she watched birds and animals and studied how they lived. Jane made careful notes about the things she saw.

Evenings were for stories. Mrs. Goodall read aloud by the hour. Best of all, Jane liked Rudyard Kipling's animal tales and Tarzan's adventures. She began to dream of the faraway lands and interesting wild animals in the stories.

The older Jane got, the more she liked studying wildlife and the less she liked school. How she hated to be indoors! On the way to school Jane would stop often to look at a new bird or playful squirrel. Sometimes she was late. Then she would hide until the first class was over. But the teacher always saw Jane's red beret through the bushes.

Finally Mrs. Goodall told Jane that she must be a better student.

Jane frowned. "Why do I have to go to school at all?" she asked. "Why can't I go to Africa and study animals?"

"You can," her mother an-

swered. "But the first thing is to get good grades in school. Then you can become a scientist. Only scientists can go to Africa and study animals."

With a sigh Jane said, "Then I might as well get it over with. I'll try not to be late anymore," she promised. "And I'll even work hard at every subject—whether I like it or not."

From then on Jane began to get better grades. After school she still climbed her favorite tree, roamed over the cliffs, and walked along the shore. She brought home birds' nests and eggs, turtles, insects, seashells, and skulls of small animals.

One day Jane heard that a farm for old horses needed money, and she wanted to help. In a sunny corner of the backyard Jane laid out her nature collection. She put up a sign that said: NATURAL HISTORY MUSEUM. ALL CONTRIBUTIONS FOR OLD HORSES.

For three summers Jane's museum earned money for the farm.

Next, Jane wrote a weekly newspaper about everything from the tiniest insect to the largest animal. Mrs. Goodall typed *The Alligator* and made copies for Judy and Jane's friends.

Jane finished high school with honors. But she could not become a scientist yet. Her parents had separated, and there was no money for an expensive university education. Instead, Jane went to a school for secretaries. She got a job with a movie company in London.

"I haven't given up," she told her mother. "Somehow I'll get to Africa and study animals."

"It's up to you," Mrs. Goodall said. "If you want something badly enough, you must fight for it."

Three long years passed. Most of the time Jane felt like two people. One Jane did office work and learned how to splice and edit film. The other Jane longed to be outdoors.

One spring day a letter came from an old school friend who

lived in Kenya. She asked Jane to come for a visit. This was the chance Jane had been waiting for. Kenya was an African country famous for its wild animals. Her hopes rose, then fell. Where could she get the money for a plane ticket to Kenya? Her small salary was only enough for food and rent.

Jane telephoned the news to her mother. "I think you ought to go," Mrs. Goodall said. "Come home and work here. Then you can save every penny you earn."

Jane made up her mind to do it. But how long would it take? Months? Years?

It took only one summer. Every day Jane worked long hours in a Bournemouth restaurant. She scraped together enough money for a plane ticket to Kenya. For good luck, Jane stuffed her old toy, Jubilee, into her suitcase.

In 1957, when Jane was twenty-three, she stepped out of the plane onto African soil. On the drive to her friend's farm she saw for the first time giraffes, elephants, and zebras in their own world. She never forgot the thrill of that day.

Although it was fun living on the farm, Jane could think of only one thing—how she could study wild animals. Soon she moved to Nairobi, the capital of Kenya. Perhaps someone there could help her.

Then Jane did something that changed her life. She went to see Dr. Louis Leakey, a famous scientist who worked in the museum. He and his wife had spent many years in Africa studying man's ancestors. Jane told him what she wanted to do. He listened; he smiled. "I think I have a job for you," he said. "Would you like to be my secretary?"

"Wonderful!" Jane said happily. In a few days she started working in what is now called the National Museum of Natural History of Kenya. An exciting new world opened for Jane. She

learned about anthropology, the
study of man; and paleontology,
the study of fossils.

Later she traveled with the Leakeys to Olduvai Gorge in Tanzania. She helped them search for bones and skulls that were more than a million years old. Dr. Leakey believed that some of the fossils belonged to early man. From dawn to dusk Jane picked carefully at the crumbling rock.

She never complained about the burning heat and backbreaking labor.

On the way to Nairobi, Dr. Leakey told Jane about a group of chimpanzees that lived on the shores of Lake Tanganyika in Tanzania. "Someone should study those chimps before it is too late," he said. "Man is rapidly taking their land. Also, a study of chimps in the wild might help scientists understand ancient man."

After a pause, Dr. Leakey said, "Jane, I believe you could do it. Would you like to try?"

For a moment Jane did not speak. She could hardly believe what she had heard. Then she cried, "Oh, yes! It's what I've always wanted to do."

The idea of living in the bush thrilled Jane. She was ready to set out for Lake Tanganyika the very next day. But it was not that simple. First she had to find

someone to pay her expenses. Jane wrote a stream of letters to institutions that help scientists. Most of them would not give money to Jane because she did not have a university degree.

She returned to England. Month after month she waited. She was afraid her dream would not come true after all. At last the Wilkie Foundation sent enough money to buy equipment and supplies for six months. But then there was a new problem. The government of Tanzania would not let her go alone into the jungle. And none of Jane's friends wanted to live in such a wild, faraway place. Finally Mrs. Goodall came to Jane's rescue. She would go with her daughter.

Jane began her long and re-warding adventure in 1960. She and her mother bounced over eight hundred miles of rough roads to Kigoma, on the shore of Lake Tanganyika. Here they bought supplies and hired a cook, Dominic. A boat took them the last twelve miles of their jour-ney. Jane's small dinghy bobbed along behind them. It would be her only link with Kigoma and the outside world.

Jane's first glimpse of Gombe, the chimpanzee area, made up for all the waiting. Thick jungle plants grew down to the beach and covered the steep inland peaks. Jane thought it was a beautiful spot. But Mrs. Goodall se-

cretly worried about the disease-
carrying insects and dangerous
wild animals.

While some curious Africans
watched, Dominic put up two
tents and unpacked the equipment. That first night Jane pulled

her camp cot out underneath the stars. Already she knew that this would be her favorite place in the whole world. Somehow Jane felt that she had been born to live and work here.

The first few months African bush experts taught Jane a great deal about the area. It was exciting when Jane finally went exploring alone. But it was disappointing, too. Day after day Jane got up before dawn and hiked for miles without getting close to a single chimpanzee. There were bushpigs, banded mongooses, squirrels, shrews, monkeys, and baboons—but no chimps. Some-

times Jane heard their loud hoot-
ing or saw one vanish into the
bush. Even when she climbed to
her lookout spot, the Peak, Jane
saw no chimps. She was puzzled.
What was she doing wrong?
Would she never get close
enough to study them?

Mrs. Goodall was a great help during those difficult weeks. She kept the camp neat and running smoothly. She added to Jane's collection of insects and plants. Africans came to get medicines from her clinic. They soon became friends. But most important, Mrs. Goodall gave Jane hope and encouragement. If she found jungle life hard, she never said so. In the evenings Mrs. Goodall told funny stories about her day in camp to make Jane laugh.

Years later Jane said, "How lucky I was to have a mother like her—a mother in a million! I could not have done it without her."

At the end of three months both Jane and her mother fell ill with malaria. They were not strong enough for the boat trip to see the doctor in Kigoma, so Dominic took care of them. He was a good nurse. In a few weeks his patients were up and about again.

It was on Jane's first day out of bed that she got a close look at chimpanzees. She had managed to climb to the Peak when several groups paid her a visit. It was the turning point for Jane. The next morning she carried a small tin trunk up to her lookout.

It contained some coffee, a kettle, cans of beans, a sweater, and a blanket. Whenever the chimps slept in tree nests near the Peak, Jane spent the night there, too.

As the weeks went by, the chimps began to accept the slim blond young woman who liked to sit near them so quietly. Jane gave names to her regular visitors. There was old Mr. McGregor with his balding head. Jane

knew Flo by her raggedy ears and large nose. Flo's baby, Fifi, was always clinging to her mother. Olly had a fluff of hair on the back of her neck. The two males Jane saw most often were David Greybeard and big, strong Goliath.

At the end of the first five months Mrs. Goodall returned to England. Jane stayed in Gombe another year. Although she missed her mother, she never felt lonely in the bush. Africans gave her their friendship, as well as valuable assistance in her work. And Jane had many bird and animal visitors. Even at night when Jane stayed up late to type notes, she had company. Terry, the toad, came to gorge on insects that fluttered around the lamp. Crescent, the genet, dropped in for a banana. Jubilee, the toy chimp, was always there in his camp chair.

Rain or shine, Jane studied the chimpanzees. "The only sure way of finding out how an animal really lives and behaves," she said, "is to watch an individual or group for long periods of time." Jane made some important discoveries. She was the first per-

son to see wild chimps eat meat
and use "tools." They stripped
twigs and stuck them into termite
mounds to pull out the tasty insects. They made sponges out of
leaves to sop up water from a hol-

low place. Jane was especially interested to see how Flo and the other mothers raised their young.

Living in the jungle was not always pleasant. Jane had to endure insect bites and the malaria fever that came back in the rainy season. Poisonous cobras, hungry leopards, and angry male chimpanzees sometimes frightened her. But she accepted the hardships and danger. They were part of the life she had chosen.

Now the National Geographic Society was paying for Jane's research. However, she had to get more scientific education. In December, 1961, Jane returned to England to study at Cambridge

University. The next spring she was back again in Gombe to continue her work.

This time she was not alone for long. The National Geographic sent Baron Hugo Van Lawick to Gombe to film the chimpanzees. He was at once drawn to Jane. They fell in love and were married in London in 1964.

For five years Jane spent almost every winter at Cambridge and summers in Africa with Hugo. It was a proud moment for her when she received a Doctor of Philosophy degree in ethology, the study of animal behavior.

By 1965 Jane's work had become so important that a permanent camp was built at Gombe. Scientists and students traveled

there to work and study. Today it
is a busy research center. Thanks
partly to Jane's efforts, the chimpanzee area was made a national

park. She hoped that her animal
friends would always have a safe
place to live.

Jane gave birth to a son, Hugo,
in 1967. She nicknamed him
"Grub" ("bush baby" in Swahili).
Soon Jane was at Gombe only
three months out of the year. The
rest of the time she and Grub
were on safari with Hugo while
he filmed the lion, cheetah,
hyena, leopard, jackal, and wild
dog. Jane helped by writing
about the lives of these animals.

Using her notes from Gombe, Jane wrote her first book, *In the Shadow of Man*. She and Hugo wrote *Grub the Bush Baby* and *Innocent Killers*. Hugo's photographs illustrate the books. During these years the Van Lawick marriage became unhappy. Jane and Hugo were divorced in 1974.

With Grub by her side, Jane continued to study the behavior of wild animals in Africa. Grub became a friend to many of the chimps and baboons. Sometimes

Hugo filmed animals for their television series.

Jane and her toy chimp, Jubilee, have come a long way since that day in the hen house. Now a famous scientist, Dr. Goodall has received several awards for her research. She is also known all over the world as one who cares about animals. Her time is divided between the Gombe she loves and the universities of Palo Alto, California and Dar es Salaam in Tanzania where she teaches and does laboratory research.

The story of Jane Goodall is not over. Many more years are needed to complete her studies. She especially hopes that her research on chimpanzee behavior will shed

light on the behavior of our
Stone-Age ancestors.

"In a way," she says, "my work
is just beginning."

About the Author

Eleanor Coerr grew up in Saskatchewan, Canada. After she received a BA from the American University in Washington, D.C., she began to write newspaper columns for children. She has traveled widely and started the first public library for children in Ecuador, a project which prompted her to get an MA in library science.

Ms. Coerr has written three previous books for Putnam's. These are the two nature biographies *Biography of a Giant Panda* and *Biography of a Kangaroo* and the See and Read Storybook *The Mixed-up Mystery Smell*.

About the Artist

Kees de Kiefte is a well-loved illustrator in both the United States and Europe, having numerous books to his credit.

He lives in Nieuwkoop, Holland, with his wife, Emmy, and his two sons, Oskar and Caspar. This is his first book for Putnam.